DIGGING UP THE PAST

TROY *and*
KNOSSOS

PETER HICKS

RSVP
RAINTREE
STECK-VAUGHN
PUBLISHERS
The Steck-Vaughn Company

Austin, Texas

DIGGING UP THE PAST
Biblical Sites • Bodies from the Past • Pompeii and Herculaneum • The Search for Dinosaurs • Troy and Knossos • The Valley of the Kings

Cover background: The Bull Portico of Knossos—the Palace of King Minos—is decorated by the famous bull fresco.

Cover inset: The Late Minoan bull's head rhyton, or drinking vessel, found at Knossos

Title page: The legend of the Trojan War, and the trick played by the Greeks to enter the city inside a hollow wooden horse, has been a popular story since ancient times. This 670 B.C. clay jar has a carving depicting soldiers inside the Trojan Horse.

Contents page: Sir Arthur Evans is famous as the archaeologist who excavated and restored much of Knossos.

Published by Raintree Steck-Vaughn Publishers, an imprint of Steck-Vaughn Company

Library of Congress Cataloging in Publication Data
Hicks, Peter, 1952–
    Troy and Knossos / Peter Hicks.
    p.   cm.—(Digging up the past)
    Includes bibliographical references and index.
    Summary: Describes the Aegean civilizations and the archaeological efforts to excavate the ancient cities of Troy and Knossos.
    ISBN 0-8172-4523-5
    1. Troy (Extinct city)—Juvenile literature.
    2. Knossos (Extinct city)—Juvenile literature.
    [1. Troy (Extinct city) 2. Knossos (Extinct city)]
    I. Title. II. Series: Digging up the past
DF221.T8H53   1996   95-40000

Printed in Italy
1 2 3 4 5 6 7 8 9 0 00 99 98 97 96

Picture acknowledgments
The author and publisher would like to thank the following for allowing their photographs to be reproduced in this book: Archiv für Kunst und Geschichte (AKG London Ltd.) *cover inset* (© E. Lessing), *title page* (© E. Lessing), 6–7, 17, 19 (both),
22 (top) (© E. Lessing), 40 (© E. Lessing), 42 (© E. Lessing), 44 (center, bottom right); Ashmolean Museum, Oxford University 28, 37; E. T. Archive 8 (Victoria and Albert Museum), 12 (National Archaeological Museum, Naples); C. M. Dixon 14, 25, 30–31(Heraklion Museum), 32 (top right), 32 (top left) (Heraklion Museum), 33 (Heraklion Museum), 39 (Heraklion Museum), 43 (top) (British Museum), 45 (right); Sonia Halliday 22 (bottom) (© F. H. C. Birch); Robert Harding 31, 34 (© M. Short); Michael Holford 5 (British Museum), 6 (British Museum), 7 (top) (British Museum), 36, 41(top) (British Museum), 43 (bottom) (British Museum); Hulton Deutsch Collection *contents page*, 11, 15, 16, 18, 20, 21 (top), 27, 29; Topham (Picture Point) *cover background*, 26, 30, 32 (bottom), 35 (both), 38 (Topham Picture Source), 41 (bottom), 44 (top left), 45 (left); W.P.L. 21 (bottom), 23 (top) (© University of Cincinnati).
All artwork is by Peter Bull Art Studio.

Contents

The Aegean Civilizations

Setting the Scene

This map shows the Aegean region and many of the important sites mentioned in this book. ▼

The wonderful Greek world that flourished after 2000 B.C. is regarded by many as marking the beginning of European civilization. The mainland Greeks were good farmers, sailors, and traders who settled the many islands of the Aegean Sea. This extraordinary Bronze Age civilization was to produce great achievements in literature, art, theater, and philosophy.

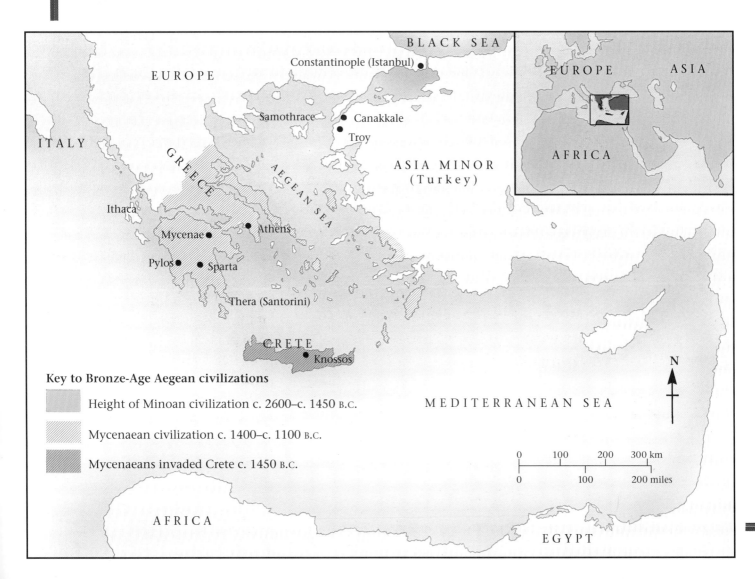

Key to Bronze-Age Aegean civilizations

Height of Minoan civilization c. 2600–c. 1450 B.C.

Mycenaean civilization c. 1400–c. 1100 B.C.

Mycenaeans invaded Crete c. 1450 B.C.

The Minoans and the Mycenaeans

Interestingly, the first civilization in the Aegean region was not on the Greek mainland, but on the narrow, rocky island of Crete. This is known as the Minoan civilization after one of its legendary kings—King Minos. The island's fertile soil produced plentiful supplies of wheat, olive oil, and wine, and by trading with other islands the Minoans became wealthy. Many fine palaces were built, such as those at Knossos, Phaistos, and Zakro. The Minoan civilization flourished for over one thousand years until two disasters struck. Around 1500 B.C. the volcanic island of Thera, 60 miles north of Crete, erupted. Huge tidal waves flooded parts of Crete, drowning many coastal towns forever, while violent earthquakes badly damaged the palace at Knossos. The second disaster for the Minoans came later—around 1450 B.C.— when the warlike Mycenaeans from the Greek mainland invaded and conquered Crete.

The Mycenaeans in turn created a rich and powerful state, building an impressive trading network in the Aegean region. Not surprisingly, trade competition sometimes led to wars with neighboring states. The Mycenaeans had an impressive army equipped with bronze armor and weapons. However, in time, the city-state of Mycenae became weaker and easy prey to tribes from the north. By 1100 B.C. Greece had entered a confused period of its history known as the "Dark Ages."

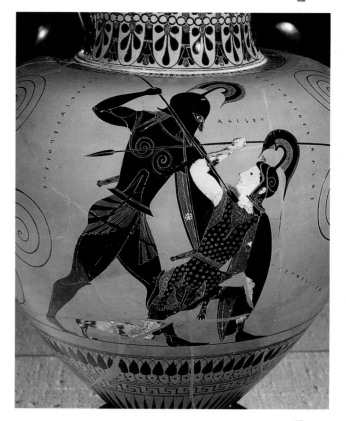

▲ Achilles (left) in battle with the Amazon queen Penthesileia. Achilles was a Mycenaean Greek hero who featured in the legend of the Trojan War (see page 7). This tale caught the imagination of the ancient world, and its events were often shown on vases and bowls.

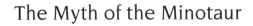

The Myth of the Minotaur

By the eighth century B.C., Greece had developed a great tradition of storytelling—a mythology—that was passed on from generation to generation by word of mouth. Many of these stories were set in the Bronze Age.

One tale told of Minos, the fierce king of Crete. In revenge for the killing of his son by the Greeks, Minos demanded that fourteen young Athenians (from the Greek city-state of Athens) be sacrificed every nine years to a terrible monster. The monster was called the Minotaur, a half-man, half-bull creature who lived in a maze, called the Labyrinth, beneath Minos's palace. The king of Athens, named Aegeus, had a son, Theseus, who volunteered to go as one of the fourteen Athenians in order to slay the Minotaur. After many adventures Theseus succeeded in killing the Minotaur, and he returned to Athens. It had been agreed that if Theseus survived, white sails would be used on the return journey and this would be a sign for the waiting King Aegeus that his son was alive. In all the excitement, the black sails had not been replaced and Aegeus, thinking his son was dead, threw himself into the sea and drowned. The sea in which this is said to have happened is called the Aegean in his name.

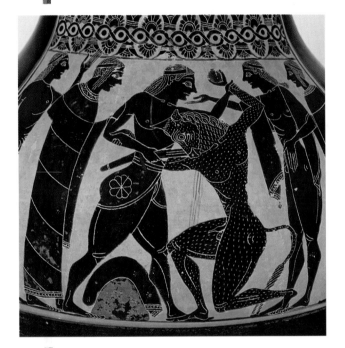

▲ Theseus killing the Minotaur. The legend of Theseus and the Minotaur tells us that Theseus found his way to the center of the dark Labyrinth by following an unraveled ball of string, provided by Ariadne, the daughter of King Minos.

Homer—The *Iliad* and the *Odyssey*

▲ The blind poet Homer. We know very little about him, and seven Greek cities claim to be his birthplace.

▼ A fifth-century B.C. bowl showing scenes from the Trojan War. Paintings such as this give us a good idea what weapons and armor were like in ancient warfare

The Greek poet Homer is thought to have lived in the mid-eighth century B.C. Homer is famous for two great epic poems, the *Iliad* and the *Odyssey*. He used to recite the poems, perhaps to music, and they were handed down through the centuries. They were not put in writing until much later. The *Iliad* tells of part of a terrible war that lasted for ten years between the Greek city-state of Mycenae and the city of Troy in Asia Minor (modern-day Turkey). It was said the war began when Paris, the son of the Trojan king, Priam, stole Helen, the wife of Menelaus, king of the Greek city-state of Sparta. The story of how the Greeks sneaked into Troy by a trick is referred to in the *Odyssey*. The Greeks pretended to go away, but left a huge wooden horse outside the walls of the city. The Trojans, thinking it was a gift, brought it inside and began celebrating their victory. In the night, Greek soldiers crept out of the hollow horse and opened the gates for their returning army, which destroyed Troy by burning it to the ground. The *Odyssey* also tells the story of the terrible obstacles that Odysseus—a Greek leader—had to overcome to get home after the war.

The Trojan War legend has had an important impact on our civilization. Not only has it appeared in many plays and books, but also in everyday speech. We talk of a person's weak spot as an "Achilles' heel," a long journey as an "odyssey," and use the expression "beware of Greeks bearing gifts." This book is the story of the archaeologists who were obsessed by these wonderfully vivid tales and wanted to prove that the tales were more than just legend and had some basis in truth and history.

SECTION 1:
The Search for Troy

Homer's magnificent stories of the Trojan War were never forgotten. The ancient Greeks and Romans saw it as a real event. Great leaders and generals, including Alexander the Great (356–323 B.C.), visited the supposed site of the siege, then known as Ilion, for inspiration. It is even thought that Julius Caesar (100–44 B.C.) visited Troy—named New Ilium in Roman times— and promised to rebuild it as the capital of the Roman Empire.

The Written Tale

At some point after the sixth century B.C., the poems about the Trojan War were written down on papyri to be copied and preserved for the future. The stories caught the imagination of the ancient world and huge numbers of copies were made. More than half the scraps of papyri found by archaeologists in Egypt up to 1939 were copies of the *Iliad* and the *Odyssey*. The tales of the war were retold during Roman times and for hundreds of years after the fall of the Roman Empire in A.D. 476. Around 1160 a French writer, Benoît de Sainte-Maure, wrote a version of the story in which he changed the events of the war to suit the age in which he lived, with the main heroes on horseback in shining armor.

This tapestry, made in A.D. 1475–1490, depicts the Trojan War. It shows the ancient Greek and Trojan armies in medieval-style armor and garments. Medieval versions of the Trojan War story were very popular. ▼

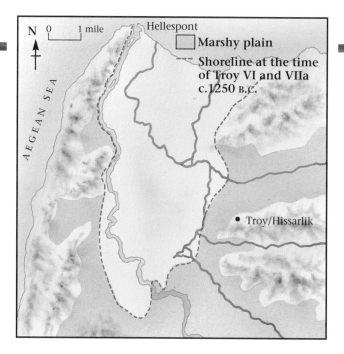

This map shows the position of Troy on the Hissarlik plain.

The exact location of Troy (or Ilium) was lost, and over the centuries the site was buried under many layers of earth. But many travelers in the Medieval period searched for it. One traveler, Cyriac of Ancona, believed that Homer's geographical descriptions were accurate. If Troy was sited on a wide plain near the Hellespont, near a fast-flowing river, and visible from the island of Samothrace, this would place the city somewhere in the northwest corner of Asia Minor (Turkey).

By the eighteenth century many scholars were trying to pin down the precise location of Troy, and it was generally felt that patient field work would sooner or later reveal Homer's city. A crucial contribution to the search came in 1822 when Charles Maclaren published his *Dissertation on the Topography of the Plain of Troy*. In this he claimed that Troy was hidden near the mound of Hissarlik, in Turkey. However, because Maclaren had never visited the site, his theory was ignored for many years.

One man who had read Maclaren's ideas was Frank Calvert. He was the American Vice-Consul at Çanakkale, in Turkey, between 1859 and 1879, and he was very interested in archaeology and the poems of Homer. By the 1860s he became more and more certain that Troy was near Hissarlik, which is Turkish for "the place of the fort."

Calvert managed to buy a section of land at Hissarlik and began a small excavation in 1865, when he dug four trial trenches. Trial trenches are dug by archaeologists across a suspected site to see if they reveal anything of interest. Calvert discovered the classical Temple of Athena (the patron goddess of New Ilium) and the impressive walls built by Lysimachus, Alexander the Great's general, in the fourth century B.C. Calvert also hit Bronze Age levels below the temple. This modest dig was very useful, for it showed that Hissarlik was an extremely complicated site, with a highly complex stratigraphy. It would need plenty of care, patience, and money to excavate properly.

A cross section plan of the different layers of the site of Troy, which are discussed in this book. ▼

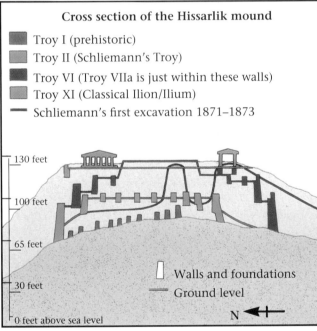

Cross section of the Hissarlik mound

■ Troy I (prehistoric)
■ Troy II (Schliemann's Troy)
■ Troy VI (Troy VIIa is just within these walls)
■ Troy XI (Classical Ilion/Ilium)
— Schliemann's first excavation 1871–1873

130 feet
100 feet
65 feet
30 feet
0 feet above sea level

☐ Walls and foundations
— Ground level

N ◄┼

Layer by Layer

Stratigraphy is a very important technique in archaeology. Sites are often built up of layers, or strata, as time passes. This means that the oldest layers are at the bottom and the most recent are near the top. We now know that the mound at Hissarlik has 56 feet of deposits. Its nine main layers and 47 subdivisions, representing over 4,000 years of history, make Troy a complicated archaeological problem.

Frank Calvert was not a wealthy man and although he owned some of Hissarlik, he could not provide the huge organization and resources required for a major dig. Because of this, Calvert's name is rarely remembered as the discoverer of Troy. It was German millionaire Heinrich Schliemann who was to win the fame for discovering Homer's long-lost city.

Schliemann's Troy

The man who was to capture the world's imagination with his archaeological exploits came from fairly humble origins. Heinrich Schliemann was born near Mecklenburg in Germany in 1822, the son of a preacher and the fifth child of nine brothers and sisters. He began working as an apprentice grocer, but was let go because of poor health. He then traveled to Amsterdam, in the Netherlands, where he quickly learned the business of buying and selling goods. Schliemann was naturally good at languages and he learned English, Dutch, French, Russian, Spanish, Italian, and Portuguese. These language skills helped him develop a good reputation as an importer and exporter of goods. By 1846, he was living in Russia and was the St. Petersburg representative of B. H. Schroder, a powerful European merchant bank. Schliemann was dealing in goods such as tea, coffee, and German wine.

▲ Heinrich Schliemann, businessman, self-made millionaire, and archaeologist. During his life he was also accused of being a liar and a thief. This photograph was taken the year he began excavating at Hissarlik.

Schliemann's Fortune

In 1850 Schliemann left for the United States, where he began to make his vast fortune. His visit coincided with the California Gold Rush. With his unfailing gift for making a profit, Schliemann bought and sold nearly $1,400,000 worth of gold dust. He was forced to leave the country very suddenly; it was rumored he was involved in some illegal gold dealings. After a dangerous journey through Panama, Central America, he arrived back in St. Petersburg in 1852 a very wealthy man.

However, the Crimean War (1853–1856) between Russia and the allied powers of Great Britain, France, and Turkey made Schliemann even richer. War often benefits traders because certain goods are in short supply. By good luck, Schliemann managed to corner the market in materials such as saltpeter, sulfur, and lead, used to make gunpowder, bullets, and guns. These were essential for Russia's war effort. He doubled his fortune in a single year.

Again, Schliemann made even more money out of the shortages—particularly cotton—caused by the U.S. Civil War (1861–1865). But suddenly, in 1864, the multimillionaire decided to close down his business operations and embark on a world tour. It was this experience that would bring him in touch with archaeology and ultimately lead him to Troy.

This first century A.D. Roman mosaic was found at Pompeii, Italy. It depicts the battle at Issus, Turkey, in 333 B.C., between the Greek army of Alexander the Great (left, on horseback) and the Persian army led by King Darius (in the chariot). The excavation of Pompeii in the 1860s inspired Schliemann to find and explore an ancient site for himself. ▼

Interest in Archaeology—or Glory?

In 1868, Schliemann visited Pompeii, the Roman town destroyed and covered by the volcanic eruption of Vesuvius in A.D. 79. This archaeological site had just recently been rescued from the ravages of treasure hunters. Giuseppe Fiorelli had organized the excavation of the site on a scientific basis and imposed order on what had been chaos. Schliemann noted in his diary that the excavations took place at great speed. It could be that seeing such a successful dig made him wish to achieve the same results at his own site.

He soon had an opportunity to try his hand at practical archaeology. Later that year he arrived in Ithaca, the Greek island home of legendary Odysseus. Schliemann hired three laborers and immediately set out to find the Greek hero's palace. At the top of Mount Aëtos, while digging for Odysseus's bedchamber with a pickax, Schliemann uncovered 20 vases and managed to break 15 of them. Holding one vase containing ashes, he wondered whether he had found the remains of Odysseus and his wife, Penelope. This is one of the many times Schliemann made evidence fit his own theories— a very unscientific practice.

▲ Schliemann also tried to find evidence of the Greek leader Agamemnon on mainland Greece. In this photograph Schliemann (bottom right) is standing by the Lion Gate, at Mycenae.

Excavating six tombs at Mycenae, Greece, Schliemann found a beautiful gold mask. He claimed it was the "face of Agamemnon." Later it was found that, not only was the mask from a much older period than that of Homer's famous king, but also, some archaeologists believe that Schliemann added the mustache to make the face look more kingly! ▶

Schliemann Moves from Greece to Turkey

Schliemann then moved on to Athens in order to plan his quest for Troy. At this time he accepted the view of some scholars that Pinarbasi, southwest of Hissarlik, was the site of Troy. But, when he traveled to Turkey in August, he was not impressed when he arrived at Pinarbasi, describing it as a "dirty village of 23 hovels." On August 15, 1868, a crucial meeting took place between Schliemann and Frank Calvert. Calvert eagerly told Schliemann of his theories and his excavations at Hissarlik, hoping to win the support of this rich benefactor. Schliemann agreed with Calvert and excitedly bombarded him with questions about the possibility of excavation. It might have occurred to Calvert that Schliemann was taking Calvert's ideas about Hissarlik and making them his own.

Schliemann Starts Work at Hissarlik

Schliemann began a small-scale exploratory dig in April 1870, but one obstacle remained between Schliemann and his dream of excavating the mound at Hissarlik. This was permission from the Turkish government. The Turks were becoming very concerned about preserving as many of their archaeological remains as possible. When they did grant Schliemann his permit, they applied strict rules. These were: any finds were to be divided between him and the new Turkish archaeological museum in Constantinople (modern-day Istanbul); all parts of the site were to be left as they were found and nothing was to be demolished; and all excavations were to be paid for by Schliemann. Of all these conditions, only the last was met.

The dig that Schliemann began in 1871 was not only a milestone in archaeology, it was also the beginning of a bitter feud with the

Turkish government. People such as Frank Calvert, who knew the site, suggested that Hissarlik should be carefully excavated with small trenches. Calvert knew the mound was very complex, so care and patience would be required. Schliemann did not agree. He believed that Homer's Troy would be the oldest layer and therefore the deepest. Schliemann—an inexperienced archaeologist—was about to dig blindly through complex stratification that he did not really understand.

▲ Eager to prove he had found more evidence of the remains of the Trojan War heroes, Schliemann claimed that a burial mound near the Hellespont was the tomb of Achilles.

Methods, Mistakes, and Deceptions

Schliemann was to excavate Hissarlik during five separate campaigns, but the second one of 1871–1873 was to be the most famous. He appeared to be a well-organized archaeologist, bringing in the best digging equipment from Great Britain and keeping a detailed diary containing a record and sketches of all the finds. The diaries tell us of the large numbers of workers on the site, which varied from 80 to 160 at a time.

▲ Schliemann's excavations at Troy. He dug quickly and carelessly, and reached the remains of the earliest cities—Troy I (3000–2500 B.C.) and Troy II (2500–2200 B.C.)—digging right through the remains of Homer's Troy.

However, Schliemann's methods of excavation at Hissarlik were brutal to say the least. To get to the level of Homer's Troy he dug a large trench through the entire mound. This method was very destructive; it is easy to criticize Schliemann for that. His unceasing drive downward destroyed important later buildings and crucial historical evidence. He was attacked by scholars at the time and since, but in his defense it has to be said that never before had such a complicated site been excavated. Because of this Schliemann was bound to make mistakes. On his way through the mound he destroyed the foundations of a large building—his reason being that he thought it was built later than the time of Homer and therefore was in the way.

The deeper the excavations went, the more confused and depressed Schliemann became. According to his diary, he despaired of ever finding Troy and even considered giving up. Also, there was always a risk that the deep trenches might collapse. Some workers had a narrow escape when they were nearly buried by falling earth. It was all becoming too much for Schliemann.

First Finds

However, the quality of finds gradually improved. Decorated pottery, skeletons, and, on Frank Calvert's land, a wonderful marble bas-relief sculpture of the Greek god Apollo with four horses was uncovered. This find once again brought out Schliemann's ruthless streak. Calvert allowed Schliemann access to his land on the understanding that all finds would be split between them. It was clear the Apollo marble was priceless. Despite this Schliemann wanted the ends cut off for easy transportation! Calvert objected, so Schliemann smuggled the intact piece to Athens without getting permission from the Turkish authorities. It was then obvious that Schliemann was going to keep all the valuable finds for himself and not honor his agreements with Calvert or the Turkish government.

A drawing of the ruins of "Priam's Palace," which appeared in Schliemann's Atlas of Trojan Antiquities, published in 1874. ▼

By 1873 Schliemann's work was beginning to appear more promising. Was he at last getting closer to Homer's Troy? He uncovered a defensive wall, an altar for sacrifices, a road, a gateway, and a small building. Schliemann immediately called this Homer's Troy, the home of the Trojan king, Priam. His proud announcement was met with a fairly cool reception by scholars around the world.

The "Treasure of Priam"

However, at the end of May, a discovery was made that caught the imagination of the world. This was the so-called "Treasure of Priam," which Schliemann unexpectedly dug up just two weeks before he was to finish digging at Hissarlik forever.

The "Treasure" consisted of huge copper bowls (Schliemann thought they were shields), bronze, gold, silver, and electrum cups, and a hoard of copper spearheads. There was also a collection of superb jewelry that Schliemann named "The Jewels of Helen." They consisted of 8,750 tiny gold rings, bracelets, 60 earrings, a headband, and, most splendid of all, two diadems (jeweled headdresses), one made up of 16,000 gold pieces threaded on fine gold wire. The fact that he found these articles all together suggested to Schliemann that they had been gathered hastily in the face of a disaster such as fire or attack. He believed that this was the wealth of the Trojan court hidden away while the Greeks sacked the city.

▲ Schliemann was convinced he had found the hastily buried "Treasure of Priam." Here the treasure is on full display.

◄ One of a pair of earring pendants found in Troy and worn by Schliemann's wife, Sophie.

Sophie Schliemann (1852–1932) posing as "Helen of Troy," wearing the famous headdress and jewelry. Schliemann always enclosed this photograph in his letters to relatives and close friends. ▼

Stealing "The Jewels of Helen"

Critics have suggested that the pieces were discovered over a period of time and then assembled for the dramatic find. For Schliemann the most important thing was to keep the treasure a secret from the Turks so it could be smuggled to Athens. When the members of the government found that they had been tricked they were understandably very angry. They asked the Greek government to try to get the jewels back. Schliemann had hidden them carefully, so they tried to confiscate his home and furniture instead. The dispute was settled in 1875 when Schliemann paid the Turks for the jewels, although he paid only one-fifth of their estimated value.

After Schliemann—Dörpfeld's triumph

What had Schliemann's work at Hissarlik achieved? His most important discoveries were four cities at different layers under the classical settlement of Ilium. The level he called Priam's Troy was the second-lowest level and was named Troy II. He discovered its size by measuring the defensive walls—an area 660 feet by 575 feet—which made it a citadel rather than a city. Schliemann believed he had found the lost city of Homer and that the city had been rich and capable of supporting an army and defending itself.

Tragically for Schliemann, it was discovered just before his death that Troy II dated one thousand years before the traditional date of the Trojan War, which scholars had figured at 1193 B.C. or 1250 B.C. He had dug down so quickly that he had passed right through the Troy he was looking for! Schliemann's methods had caused great destruction of the site, and his ruthless behavior made other countries around the world very suspicious of foreign archaeologists who they thought might plunder treasure. Schliemann died in 1890, but his work was carried on by William Dörpfeld, a German archaeologist who had worked with him since 1882.

▲ After Schliemann's excavations, Troy was a confusing site. Here, visitors try to make sense of the different layers. The huge wall (center right) dates from Troy VI (1800–1250 B.C.) and is thought to be the remains of a palace.

◄ Schliemann's Troy II layer photographed around 1900. A look at the wide stack at the left of the picture and the scale of the figures gives a good idea of the depth that Schliemann dug from the original level of Hissarlik.

Dörpfeld Finds Troy VI

Dörpfeld's dig of 1893–1894 was also to attract much publicity. He discovered another city, now called Troy VI. This had one thousand feet of superbly built defensive wall. Interestingly, the wall was angled at the bottom, much like the one described in the *Iliad* when a Greek soldier, Achilles' friend Patroclus, tried to climb into the city. Dörpfeld also discovered defended gateways at the east and south of the city. To the west he found a somewhat weaker section of wall, which once again was consistent with a passage in Homer describing a weak point in Troy's defenses that was easy to attack.

William Dörpfeld, one of the most talented German archaeologists of all time, had the technical knowledge that Schliemann had so desperately needed. This picture of Dörpfeld was taken at Troy in 1894. ►

Inside Troy VI, Dörpfeld found the foundations of five houses. The scattered remains of Mycenaean pottery seemed to indicate that the settlement was lived in between 1500 and 1000 B.C. These dates include the traditional date of the Trojan War— thirteenth century B.C. There was also evidence of destruction—collapsed walls, piles of rubble, and even charred remains from a fire. Was this Troy the one sacked by the Mycenaean Greeks? Many scholars at the time were convinced it was, but still the evidence was not conclusive.

▲ A fourth-century B.C. Greek stone frieze, or carved scene, showing warriors during the siege of Troy

This photograph shows city walls with the base of a tower from Troy VI in the foreground. ▼

Troy VIIa—Homer's Troy?

There was a gap of 38 years before Hissarlik was again excavated. This time Carl Blegen, the head of an American team from the University of Cincinnati, Ohio, excavated, in 1932 and in 1938. His digs were among the most careful and scientific excavations in the history of archaeology. The date of the first settlement at Hissarlik is thought to be as early as 3600 B.C., and there were found to be nine cities built over each other in the mound. Blegen examined Troy VI carefully and concluded,

since the city walls had actually moved, that it had been severely damaged by an earthquake. However, on the layer above (Troy VIIa), the survivors seemed to have rebuilt among the ruins of the earthquake. The interior was overcrowded, with makeshift huts in the streets. Storage jars were set in the ground, as if the people of Troy had needed to store large amounts of food, and there was a marked shortage of imported goods. It looked as if the people were sheltering through a long siege. Ashes were everywhere—showing signs of a great fire. Bodies had been crushed by falling buildings, and some bodies showed signs of violent death. An arrowhead was uncovered near the main street. Blegen was convinced this was Homer's Troy at last.

The work carried out by Calvert, Schliemann, Dörpfeld, and Blegen at the Hissarlik site was inspired by the legend from Homer's epic poems. The excavations led to proof of an impressive Bronze Age citadel—if not of Troy itself. The implications about whether Blegen was correct or not about Troy VIIa are discussed on pages 40–41.

▲ The sunken storage jars in the floor of a house just inside the east gate. To Blegen this was evidence of food shortages and that Troy was under siege from outsiders. This layer was later called Troy VIIa (dated 1250–1180 B.C.).

An artist's impression of Troy VI (1800–1250 B.C.) from the east. ▼

Sea

Marshy plain

N

SECTION 2:
The Search for Knossos

It is not surprising that Schliemann's exploits inspired others to explore the connection between the archaeology of the Aegean and the old mythology. Many people had been fascinated by tales of the Trojan War. The same was true of the legend of the Minotaur in his lair—the Labyrinth—under the palace of King Minos on the island of Crete. For centuries travelers to this important Mediterranean island wondered where the tunnels of the Labyrinth might be. Spanish traveler Pero Tafur pinpointed the site at Knossos as early as A.D. 1435.

In the nineteenth century two Englishmen mapped the island. The first, Richard Pashley, wrote that some of the ruins reminded him of a labyrinth, but doubted whether the legend of King Minos, Theseus, and the Minotaur was more than just a story. In 1865, Thomas Spratt, a naval surveyor who had mapped the area around Troy in the 1830s, also identified the ruined site of Knossos, by the Kairatos River. He also noted that parts of the site were being robbed of stone to build houses at the nearby port of Heraklion.

A map of Minoan Crete showing some of the palaces, one of the most famous being Knossos on the north coast. Knossos is sometimes also called the Palace of Minos. ▼

SEA OF CRETE

N

CRETE

Heraklion (Iraklion)

Knossos

Sacred caves of Arkalochri

Zakro

Phaistos

0   25   50   75   100 km

0   20   40   60 miles

MEDITERRANEAN SEA

Who Found Knossos?

The man who is always connected with Knossos is British archaeologist Sir Arthur Evans, who led a famous dig between 1900 and 1905. However, just as Schliemann was not the discoverer of Troy, Evans had nothing to do with finding the location of the palace. The man who started unearthing this famous site was a Cretan named Minos Kalokairinos, a local businessman who began an excavation in 1878.

▲ Knossos seen from a distance among the hills near the modern port of Heraklion (now called Iraklion). Trading produce from fertile lands had made the Minoan civilization wealthy.

Knossos at this time was under Kefala Hill, and Kalokairinos dug twelve six-foot deep trenches and uncovered the remains of a very large building. He had found the west wing of a palace and the apartments containing the Throne Room. Kalokairinos found red painted walls and unearthed the west front of the building. He excavated a storeroom, finding twelve pithoi (large storage jars) containing barley, beans, and peas. Kalokairinos also found a clay tablet with strange inscriptions on it (see pages 30–31 and 37–39). The large amounts of pottery he excavated almost certainly belonged to the thirteenth century B.C.

This dig had been successful, but the Cretan authorities stopped any further excavation. Crete at this time was ruled by Turkey and the Cretan parliament was afraid the Turks would take the finds to a museum in Istanbul.

The Bull Portico of Knossos. The stunning architecture of the palace, with its brightly colored pillars and detailed frescoes, shows the richness of the Minoan culture. ▶

Kalokairinos sent the pithoi he had found to various centers of archaeology, such as London, Paris, and Rome, trying to attract interest in his discoveries. Both Schliemann and Dörpfeld visited the site, but perhaps not surprisingly after the problems at Troy, the Cretans would not give them permission to dig.

Sir Arthur Evans showed great interest in Knossos and he visited Kalokairinos's collection in 1894. Since Evans hoped to have the chance to dig at Knossos, he bought a quarter of Kefala Hill before going home to England. He returned to the island in 1898, just in time to witness the overthrow of Turkish power in Crete. Unfortunately, during the fighting, Kalokairinos's collection and excavation notes were destroyed. Once Crete gained its independence, Evans was able to buy the rest of Kefala Hill, and he made preparations to start excavations in March 1900.

Evans—The Careful Archaeologist

The career and personality of Sir Arthur Evans could not have been more different from that of Schliemann, the ruthless excavator of Troy. Evans was born in 1851, the son of Sir John Evans, a respected archaeologist. He went to Harrow School and then Oxford University, where he graduated with a first-class Honors Degree in History. Traveling widely, he became very interested in the Balkans, the region in southeast Europe between the Adriatic and Aegean seas, and became a newspaper reporter there. At that time the Austrian Empire controlled many of the Balkan States. Evans's reporting got him into a lot of trouble. He was imprisoned by the Austrians, who accused him of helping an uprising against their rule.

Sir Arthur Evans in 1936, helping to prepare an exhibition of Minoan artifacts in London. He is holding a copy of the bull's head rhyton found at the bottom of a well at Knossos. ▼

After his release Evans concentrated on archaeology and was elected Keeper of the Ashmolean Museum at Oxford. He gained some practical experience of archaeology with the excavation of Frilford Roman Villa near Oxford in 1885. So whereas Schliemann was a self-made millionaire and self-taught archaeologist, Evans was born into a wealthy family and had an archaeological background. He was less flamboyant and aggressive than Schliemann, perhaps because he had already been accepted in the archaeological world.

Knossos: The 1900–1905 Excavations

The excavations that Evans directed began in March 1900 and were very well organized. He had a first-class team around him, in particular his site supervisor, a Scotsman named Duncan Mackenzie, who kept an extremely detailed logbook, or diary. Evans is regarded as one of the first scientific excavators to work in the Aegean region.

Another skill that Mackenzie possessed was his ability to get along with the local workers. The site had from 50 to 180 workers, and Mackenzie's enthusiasm kept them personally interested in the work.

Evans had seen the killing by both Christians and Muslims during the recent war for independence in Crete. Because of this he insisted that his workforce should contain workers of both religions. He felt that getting them to work together in a team was a positive way to heal the wounds between the two communities.

Both men and women were employed—the men tending to carry out the heavy digging and moving, while the women sieved the earth and cleaned and labeled the pieces of pottery. They were paid special bonuses for good work or for finding objects.

This photograph, from the Ashmolean Museum, Oxford University, shows Evans standing over the Throne Room. The picture was taken after the excavation of the Throne Room was completed in April 1901. ▼

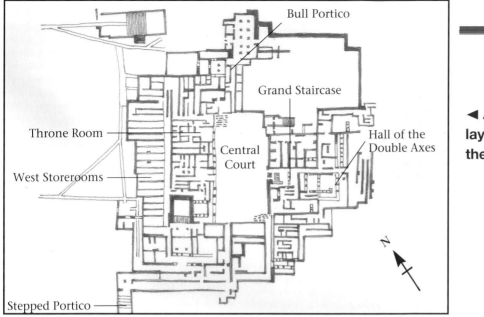

Bull Portico

Grand Staircase

Throne Room

Central Court

Hall of the Double Axes

West Storerooms

N

Stepped Portico

◄ **A diagram of the layout of Knossos, the Palace of Minos**

Money Well Spent

Evans was a very rich man, especially after he inherited his father's wealth, and this was important to the quality of the excavation. For example, it was extensively photographed at a time when photography was a fairly new and expensive technology. An observation tower was built so that photographs could be taken of the whole site. The photographs cost more than £71, a lot of money in 1902. Evans and his colleagues lodged locally at first, but later Evans had his own house built—called the Villa Ariadne, named after King Minos's daughter of the Minotaur legend who helped Theseus escape. At night in his villa, Evans wrote up his site notebooks, which contained superb sketches of the buildings and artifacts.

▲ **A long corridor, which runs west of the Throne Room, with storerooms leading off it. The two large pithoi are nearly as tall as the man.**

It was clear from the start of the excavation that Knossos was, like Troy, a very complicated site with a difficult stratigraphy. If there is one criticism that could be made of Evans it is that he dug far too quickly. A site the size of Knossos would today take many years to excavate properly.

The Throne Room

The work started on March 23, 1900, and Evans decided to dig in the area where Kalokairinos had begun in 1878. He was soon to be rewarded with an extraordinary find—the Throne Room, with the remains of frescoes and stone benches and complete with a throne in place. Scattered around in front of the throne was a large, broken pithos and four strange alabaster containers. It was essential to build a roof over the room to protect the furniture and frescoes from the weather.

The splendidly restored Throne Room, complete with a colorful fresco showing plants and the mythical griffin—a half-bird, half-lion creature. Evans thought the throne was more suitable for a woman so he called it the "Throne of Ariadne." ▶

◄ A Linear B tablet. The strange writing, known as ideograms, represents lists of rams, sheep, goats, and pigs.

Another important find came to light early on. To the south of the Throne Room was a small storeroom, containing a huge collection of clay tablets of the type Evans had seen at the home of Kalokairinos. He was to collect two thousand of these tablets, but their meaning would not be understood until many years later (see page 38), and not by Evans.

To the west of the Throne Room ran a corridor, 175 feet long, which served 21 narrow storerooms. Many contained pithoi. These massive clay jars could each hold about 40 gallons and were probably used to store olive oil, wine, grain, and beans.

Two of the 21 storerooms. Originally, they would have had roofs to keep them dark and cool to allow storage of fresh food. The darkness of the corridors and storerooms would have given the palace a mazelike appearance, not so different from the Minotaur s Labyrinth. ►

Archaeologists believe that the double ax was the most important symbol of the Minoan religion. This gold ceremonial ax, which was never intended for use, was found in the Sacred Cave of Arkalochri in central Crete. It may have been left as a gift for the gods. ▶

▲ Crude double ax symbols, or motifs, were carved into pillars and walls at Knossos.

◀ The Hall of the Double Axes. With the help of reinforced concrete, it was given a protective roof in 1928, held up by the pillars and beams in the picture.

As the members of the team progressed through the palace they found passages, impressive staircases, and a central court. Certain motifs appeared. Double axes were found on pillars, vases, and jars around the palace. One room, nearly 80 feet long, was called the Hall of the Double Axes. This is the meaning of the word *labyrinth*, which we now use to mean a maze, and the home of the mythical Minotaur.

Many of the frescoes showed charging bulls, and acrobats bull-leaping in the huge central court of the palace. The bull and Knossos were connected after all, for it looked as though the palace was the center of a bull cult. Clearly the bull was honored as a very important animal. Evans may have found the origins of the Minotaur myth.

The famous fresco depicting bull-leaping. Bull-leaping seemed to involve young men and women vaulting through a bull's horns, somersaulting, and landing on the bull's back, then leaping off. It is thought many leapers suffered serious injury and even death. ▼

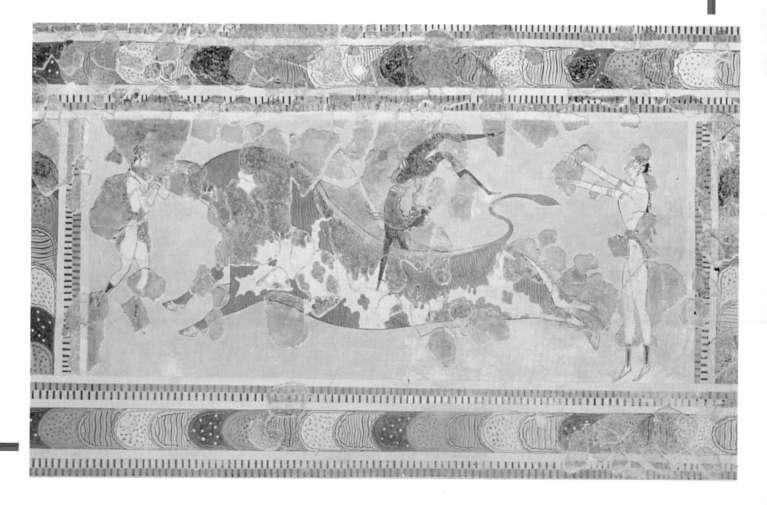

The Restoration of the Palace 1922–1930

The south entrance of the Palace of Knossos. The pillars, support-beams, and frescoes are all reconstructions built by Evans. ▼

In 1922, a young visitor to Knossos wrote in her diary that the site was "not quite a heap of stones as usual…. A great many earthenware vases and a small throne of King Minos were about the best things there!" It was because of reactions to Knossos like this one that Evans decided, in 1922, to restore some of the parts of the palace.

◄ Reinforced concrete was used to reconstruct part of this upper story in the west wing of the palace. This was a fairly new material in the 1920s, and it enabled Evans to attempt his reconstructions fairly cheaply.

What Evans did during the years 1922–1930 has long been the center of argument. His supporters say that he transformed a crumbling ruin into a marvelous reconstruction of a Minoan royal palace. Visitors feel they have traveled back in time when they experience the floors, walls, stairs, and upper stories in a state as close to their original condition as possible. In 1923 Evans finished the Stepped Portico of the Central Court, just to the south of the Throne Room. An impressive staircase was restored from a pile of slab. Similar transformations restored the Grand Staircase, with plastered and painted columns, replica frescoes, and an upper story built with reinforced concrete. The Bull Portico of the northeast entrance passage, with its charging bull fresco, is probably the most famous image of the restored Knossos.

The charging bull fresco. It is thought that many of the ceremonies and spectacles involving the bulls took place in the Central Court. ▼

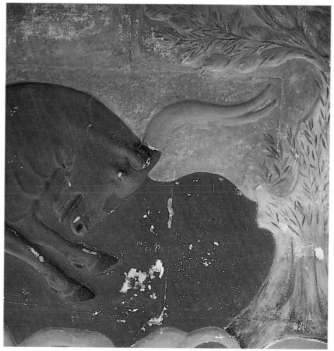

Evans's Critics

However, critics of this work say that Evans, in his attempts to impress, went too far.

Much of his restoration has been criticized as being guesswork and having no real basis in fact. It was one thing to build up ruined staircases and walls, but the authenticity of some of the rooms on upper stories is less certain. It has also been said that although Evans's restorations have not damaged the remains, they obscure them.

Had the Knossos site been excavated more recently, reconstructive models of the palace's rooms and courtyards would probably have been made and displayed in an on-site museum instead.

However, to the thousands of tourists who visit each year, a walk along the portico and then down the Grand Staircase is a thrilling experience. It is difficult to say how many visitors realize that they are walking past repainted reconstructions.

The Tablets—Linear A and B

In the first week of his excavation of Knossos Evans found large numbers of baked clay tablets with strange inscriptions on them. With the tablets were found bronze hinges, wood remains, and a type of seal, so it seems that they were kept in secure boxes. The tablets were found in the destroyed layers of a building, so they date from the destruction of Knossos. There has been a lot of argument as to when this was, but most archaeologists put it at about 1375 B.C.

Evans studied his collection of tablets carefully and tried to figure out their meaning. He seemed to recognize some of the inscriptions, but the script proved impossible to translate. However he did write in 1900 that he thought the script, which he called Linear B, "may well be some primitive form of Greek." Due to a halt of the work at Knossos during World War I (1914–1918) and the time Evans took to write up his findings of the Knossos excavations in the 1920s, he never got around to translating the tablets systematically. He did however distinguish three types of writing found on clay tablets in Crete. One, similar to Egyptian hieroglyphics, was the earliest. Another, made up of simple outlines, was called Linear A. The third and by far the most numerous script found at Knossos was Linear B.

This fragment of a Minoan offering table is inscribed with Linear A script. It is from a collection at the Ashmolean Museum, Oxford University. ▼

A Second Find of Linear B

In 1939, Carl Blegen (who had excavated at Troy) was excavating a Mycenaean palace called Pylos, on the Greek mainland. In one of the rooms he uncovered 618 tablets. Although many were damaged, it soon became clear they were written in Evans's Linear B script. World War II (1939–1945) interrupted any more work on the script, but in 1950 another 38 tablets were discovered at Mycenae. Work on the translation of Linear B did not start until 1952, when Sir John Myres, an old friend of Evans's, finally published a record of the Knossos tablets, 11 years after Evans's death.

Translated Tablets

The man who was responsible for our understanding of Linear B was an amateur in the field of ancient languages, Michael Ventris. He had been obsessed with Linear B ever since he heard a lecture by Arthur Evans as a 14-year-old in 1936. Gradually, he came to see that the script was a very early and ancient form of Greek, and that the tablets were records of goods, equipment, and even people. They were ancient stock books. Linear A still has not been translated.

▲ The man who began unlocking the mysteries of Linear B was Michael Ventris, an architect by trade. Tragically, Ventris was killed in a car crash in 1956.

The cracking of the Linear B code was important for two reasons. First, it proved that the rulers of all the Mycenaean palaces, including Knossos, spoke Greek, the language of Homer. Second, the tablets give us a great deal of information about the activities around the Aegean area that archaeology cannot provide. For example, there is no archaeological evidence that suggests flax was an important crop in the area around Pylos. However, the tablets tell us that flax and cloth production were important industries.

Detailed Records

The range and detail of information built up from the tablets is impressive. It is thought that these records were stored only for a year because there are no dates on them, only references to "this year" or "last year." Perhaps they were destroyed at the end of each year, and then a new file was begun. At Knossos we learn about details of wool production, such as the names of shepherds, the size of flocks of sheep, the amount of wool sheared, and the women who spun, wove, and decorated the woolen cloth.

There are also impressive lists of fighting strength. The most important piece of military equipment at that time was the chariot. We are told about the vehicles' bodies, their decoration and value, and the numbers of wheels and what they were made of, usually elm or willow. War equipment—armor, helmets, spears, arrows, and shields—is recorded in great detail. The lists of rowers available tell us something about naval power. These appear to have been violent times. The lists of large numbers of single women workers, called captives, who were probably slaves, point to the many wars in which these women would have been captured.

Finally, we learn about the typical diet of the time— figs, olives, wheat, wine, and pork—all listed in great detail. The secrets of these tablets were a wonderful discovery.

▲ A Linear B tablet from Knossos. It lists mainly people—men and women workers— who probably worked in the surrounding fields.

SECTION 3: Troy and Knossos: Truth or Legend?

The excavations at the two sites of Troy and Knossos were the result of hundreds of years of interest in the legends of the Trojan War and the Minotaur. What have the excavations of the last 120 years told us about the sites and where the legends come from?

This carving on a clay amphora, or jar, shows an image of the Trojan Horse with soldiers at the openings. ▼

The Legend of Troy

The Trojan War, as described in great detail by Homer, was given a traditional date of 1193 B.C. by classical scholars. The archaeologists of our story, Schliemann, Dörpfeld, and Blegen, all claimed to have found evidence of the siege and sacking of Troy. Of the three, it was actually Blegen who was most convinced. He put the date about 1250 B.C. and claimed "it can no longer be doubted that there really was an actual historical Trojan War in which a [joint force] of Achaeans, or Mycenaeans [Greeks], under a king whose overlordship was recognized, fought against the people of Troy and their allies." Critics of Blegen have argued that his finds were hardly conclusive—one arrowhead does not make a siege, and four skeletons do not prove a sacking!

Since the late 1980s, Professor Manfred Korfmann of Germany has been carrying on the work at Hissarlik and finding out more information about the various layers. However, no conclusive evidence has emerged as to whether a Trojan War ever took place. It could be that Homer did not write about an actual single war, but that he drew on various events and places from the past to weave together the wonderful tale of Troy.

The Wooden Horse

So, what of the Trojan Horse—probably the most famous incident in the legendary siege of Troy? Today, visitors to Troy can climb inside a huge modern reconstruction of the one mentioned in the *Odyssey*.

Some experts believe that the idea of the horse developed from siege engines used by soldiers of the period either to break defensive walls or to climb on top of them. Certainly such machines were used by troops in the Near East (especially the Assyrians) at this time. These were wooden towers covered in wet horsehide to prevent them from being set on fire. They sheltered dozens of armed soldiers inside. These towers are not so different from the famous Greek horse.

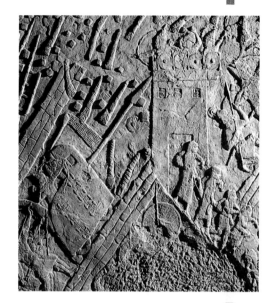

▲ An Assyrian siege engine (center) from the ninth century B.C., smashing down the walls of a city. This may have been where the idea of a Trojan Horse came from.

The Trojan Horse reconstruction built in 1974. This modern version is made from pine trees, possibly as the original was. It stands near the entrance to the site of Troy, and visitors can climb inside. ▶

The Myth from Knossos

We have seen how Evans found constant references to the bull during his excavations at Knossos and was able to learn how this animal was central to the Minoan civilization. This is not surprising, for the bull was honored for its strength, size, and fertility. From the evidence of the frescoes, bull-leaping was a celebration of this bull cult. Young men and women leaped and sometimes somersaulted over the running bulls by gripping their horns and hoisting themselves through the air. It must have required great agility and bravery. Bull-leaping is thought to have taken place in the huge courtyard at the center of the vast and complicated palace layout. At the end of the ceremony, it is believed the bulls were slaughtered.

If we piece all these facts together it is not difficult to understand how the Minotaur myth came into being. Young male and female acrobats were expected to perform incredibly dangerous leaps over running bulls. It is highly likely that many were either killed or maimed. The bull-leaping taking place at the center of a labyrinthine palace might well lead to the legend of the Minotaur and Theseus.

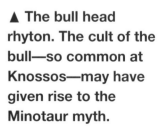

▲ The bull head rhyton. The cult of the bull—so common at Knossos—may have given rise to the Minotaur myth.

◄ This Minoan bronze statue shows a graceful, agile figure of an acrobat leaping through the horns of a charging bull. Perhaps the unsuccessful ones who died were the sources of the legends about Athenian sacrifices to the Minotaur.

Theseus's battle with the Minotaur. Myths and legends have been popular since ancient times. Archaeologists have found evidence of the possible origins of these myths. ▼

There is one final link with the legend. Evans was again working at Knossos in June 1926. His diary tells us of a small earthquake on June 26 that made the clocks stop and consisted of a wave of shocks lasting for over a minute. His villa rocked and groaned continuously and bottles were thrown off shelves. In the nearby village, dust was thrown up, and there was an uproar from the inhabitants. Listening carefully, Evans noted that "a dull sound rose from the ground like the muffled roar of an angry bull." Earthquakes have been very common throughout Cretan history, and the underground noises could have led people to tell tales of a tortured killer-bull prowling around his underground chamber.

Evans must have found the legend entertaining, but it also led him to discover an amazing Minoan civilization, and of course the Linear B tablets, which when translated, tell us so much about the Bronze Age Aegean region.

Time Line

BRONZE AGE c.2600–1000 B.C.	MODERN AGE 1822–1873

◀ **c.1950–1750 B.C.** Knossos, in Crete, is the first Minoan palace.

c.1580–1300 B.C. On the Greek mainland, Mycenaean civilization thrives.

c.1500 B.C. Volcanic island of Thera (Santorini) erupts, with serious results for Crete.

c.1450 B.C. Conquest of Crete by Mycenaeans.

c. 1375 B.C. Knossos palace destroyed.

c.1250 B.C. Possible date of the Trojan War. ▲

c.1125 B.C. Invasion of Mycenae by

1822 Charles Maclaren's *Dissertation on the Topography of the Plain of Troy* published.

1822 Heinrich Schliemann born.

1851 Sir Arthur Evans born.

1852 Schliemann arrives back in St. Petersburg, Russia, having made a fortune in the California Gold Rush.

1865 Frank Calvert begins investigations at Hissarlik.

1868 Schliemann visits Fiorelli's excavations at Pompeii, Italy.

1871 Schliemann's excavations begin at Hissarlik.

1873 Troy II uncovered. Discovery of "Priam's Treasure." ▼

This time line contains events that are important to the sites of Troy and Knossos.

MODERN AGE 1878–1930	MODERN AGE 1932–1990
1878 Minos Kalokairinos begins investigating Kefala Hill and finds ruins of Knossos.	**1932–1938** Carl Blegen's excavations at Troy. Discovers Troy VIIa (Homer's Troy).
1890 Schliemann dies.	**1941** Death of Evans.
1893–1894 William Dörpfeld discovers Troy VI.	**1945** "Treasure of Priam" disappears during the Soviet occupation of Berlin, Germany, after World War II.
1900–1905 Evans's full-scale excavations at Knossos.	**1952** Michael Ventris begins work on Linear B tablets. ▶
1922–1930 Evans begins restoration of parts of the palace at Knossos. ▼	
	1987 Professor Korfmann continues digging at Troy.
	1990 "Treasure of Priam" rumored to be hidden in the Pushkin Museum, Moscow.

Glossary

Alabaster A fine clay, usually made from gypsum, used for sculptures.

Allies Countries, or people, united to work or fight together for a particular purpose.

Assyrians Inhabitants of a great Near Eastern civilization that was powerful between 2000 and 600 B.C.

Bas-relief Sculpture carved in a flat surface so that it stands out from the background.

Bronze Age The period from c. 2600–1000 B.C., during which bronze was widely used.

Citadel A fortress that protects a city.

City-state A powerful city that has an army or fleet of ships to protect and fight for it. Ancient Greece was split into many states and city-states, such as Athens and Mycenae.

Civilization The culture or way of life of a particular people, including their arts, sciences, government, and philosophies.

Classical Having origins in ancient Greek or Roman civilization.

Confiscate To take away a person's possessions as a punishment.

Cult The honoring or worship of a particular god, person, or animal.

Dark Ages In ancient Greece, a period after 1100 B.C. when the Greek civilization broke up into warring factions and lost much of its rich culture.

Electrum An alloy of gold and silver, used in ancient times.

Epic poems Long, detailed heroic tales written down or spoken in poetic form.

Excavate To dig something from the ground.

Fertile Land that can produce a lot of plants.

Flax A grasslike plant that is used to produce linen cloth.

Frescoes Paintings made on walls while the plaster is still wet.

Hellespont The channel connecting the Sea of Marmara and the Aegean Sea. It separates Europe and Asia Minor, and is now called the Dardanelles.

Hieroglyphics An early form of writing in picture form, introduced in Egypt c. 3000 B.C.

Legend A story that has become famous and been passed down through many centuries. The word *legendary* is used when describing something connected to a legend.

Medieval Relating to a period of European history between A.D. 500 and 1500.

Minoan The Bronze Age culture of Crete from c. 2600 B.C. to c. 1350 B.C.

Mycenaeans The people from the Greek city-state of Mycenae. The Mycenaean civilization was at its most powerful c. 1400 B.C.

Myth A story that is widely known but is untrue. A *mythology* is the myths of a culture.

Papyri Paperlike materials made from a grass plant called papyrus.

Philosophy The study of knowledge in pursuit of wisdom.

Pithoi (*singular* pithos) Very large pottery storage jars.

Portico Another word for a porch—a covered entrance to a building.

State A nation, its government, and officials.

Stratification A series of layers or levels on an archaeological site.

Stratigraphy An archaeological technique involving the dating of a site by different layers.

Further Reading

Edmondson, Elizabeth. *The Trojan War*. Great Battles and Sieges. New York: New Discovery Books, 1992.

McIntosh, Jane. *Archeology*. New York: Alfred A. Knopf Books for Young Readers, 1994.

Naden, C. J. *Theseus and the Minotaur*. Legends of Ancient Greece. Mahwah, NJ: Troll Associates, 1980.

Pearson, Anne. *What Do We Know about the Greeks?* New York: Peter Bedrick Books, 1992.

Poulton, Michael. *Life in the Time of Pericles and the Ancient Greeks*. Life in the Time of.... Milwaukee: Raintree Steck-Vaughn, 1992.

Stewart, Diana, editor. *The Iliad*. Short Classics. Milwaukee: Raintree Steck-Vaughn, 1983.

Williams, A. Susan. *The Greeks*. Look into the Past. New York: Thomson Learning, 1993.

For older readers

Hamilton, Edith. *Mythology*. New York: Little, Brown & Co., 1942.

Homer. *The Iliad*. Rouse, W.H.D., translator. New York: Mentor, 1938.

Homer. *The Odyssey*. Rouse, W.H.D., translator. New York: Mentor, 1937.

Museums

United States
Los Angeles County Museum of Art
5905 Wilshire Boulevard
Los Angeles, CA 90036
(213) 857-6111

Yale University Art Gallery
1111 Chapel Street
New Haven, CT 06520
(203) 432-0600

Indiana University Art Museum
Fine Arts Building
Bloomington, IN 47405
(812) 855-5445

Walters Art Gallery
600 North Charles Street
Baltimore, MD 21201
(301) 547-9000

Museum of Fine Arts
465 Huntington Avenue
Boston, MA 02115
(617) 267-9300

The Metropolitan Museum of Art
Fifth Avenue at 82nd Street
New York, NY 10028
(212) 879-5500

The Toledo Museum of Art
2445 Monroe Street at Scottwood Avenue
Box 1013
Toledo, OH 43697
(419) 255-8000

Great Britain
The British Museum
Great Russell Street
London, WC1B 3DG
Great Britain
(0-11-44) 171-636-1555
Many of Sir Arthur Evans's finds are displayed here.

Crete
Archaeological Museum, Iraklion
Iraklion, nr Knossos
Crete
Greece
(0-11-30) 81-226092
A wonderful collection of Minoan artifacts, pottery, sculpture, and paintings.

Turkey
Istanbul Archaeological Museum
Istanbul
Turkey
(0-11-90) 21-25207740
Has many of the Schliemann, Dörpfeld, and Blegen finds from the Troy site.

Index